The Beginners Guide

to Sinning

BY

LARRY A. YFF

CHAPTERS

1. Where are we? 4

2. How did we get here? 9

3. The Manufacturer's Rules. 14

4. *It* needs a name. 22

5. Can we get rid of it? 23

6. Now what? 34

7. Private Matters 38

ACKNOWLEDGEMENTS

I want to acknowledge that everybody doesn't have the same belief system. I want to acknowledge that I think my system is better than yours and that you think yours is better than mine. I want to acknowledge that it doesn't matter whose is better or not. I want to acknowledge that you should live your life on your terms based on your beliefs. Don't look at the belief system you are about to see as being mine or yours. For best results, just view it as an option…a really, fucking good one!!

CHAPTER ONE

Where are we?

It's always important to know where you are at. That's what life's about, isn't it? We all want to get somewhere and in order to do that you first need to know where you are at. I know that sounds super simple. It's supposed to: this is the beginner's guide remember??

Let's say I want to go to Chicago. Where I am currently at makes a *huge* difference in my route. Getting to Chicago from New York is different from getting there from California. Viewing life in simple terms like that will make you a happier, successful, respectful human being.

So...we are all on a planet called Earth. Science tells us there are thousands of planets, thousands of stars and hundreds of galaxies. The most basic question you have to know before you start your day is: where am I and is this where I am supposed to be? If you can answer that simple question, your day will be off to an excellent start.

Let's get sidetracked for a second. I used to do drugs, drink Tequila, go to strip clubs or watch pornos and do drugs and drink Tequila. My drug of choice was cocaine...crack or blow. My tequila of choice was Jose Cuervo 1800 Silver. There were times when it was necessary for me to finally close my eyes the next day that I had to first figure out where was I at and is this the best place for me to be. Most times it was the absolute worst place for me. For instance, once I would partially come to my senses and realize I was in somebody's cold basement sweating profusely or in somebody's spare bedroom with my eye pupils as big as baboon nuts and that I was stuck in a trap (That's where the name "trap house" comes from, for those of you who are new to drug-game terminology. It's a place designed to drain your pockets by offering everything you need and as much of it as you need as long as you have money to spend), it was in my best interest to get the fuck out with whatever money and/or dignity I had left and get my ass home; assuming I still had a place to call home.

The main thing to remember from that trap-house example is the first step of the process: where am I? I was fortunate enough to have the option to leave one place and go to another one. We humans are on a planet called Earth with no escape. This is our home and is the best place for us. I know there are people with a whole lotta money and not a lotta common sense that want to try and make Mars or the moon our new Earth. My suggestion to them is give me some of that money because I can do a whole lot of good making Earth a better place to live with a cheaper price tag than your multi-billion dollar space projects and space ships. Always take care of home first.

Of all the thousands of planets out there, Earth is the only one we know of that has everything we need. Our bodies are made of 80% water so we need to drink water on a daily basis.

Earth is the only planet that has that. The ozone layer protects and separates air that humans can breathe from outer-space air that we cannot breathe. Earth is the only planet that has that. Trees and other green plants clean and process the chemicals in the air so we can breathe through a process called photosynthesis, and coincidentally, these plants need dirt and water, both of which are only found on good ole' planet Earth. The pull of gravity on humans is the exact amount of pressure/pull needed to be able to walk and move around. If gravity here had just a little more pull, our feet would be dragging and we wouldn't be able to walk. On the flipside, if gravity's pull was a little bit less, our feet would float higher and higher with each step and we still wouldn't be able to walk. Are you getting my point? If not, let me make it simple and clear: this planet we are on is designed for life. When I say life, I am including plant and animal life as well.

We have now successfully answered that first, critical question that will lead us towards a successful life. Now that we know where we are, it's time to figure out, in the simplest of ways, "how did we get here?"

CHAPTER TWO

How did we get here?

The 3 basic theories of how humans came into existence are 1) the Bible creation story, 2) the Big Bang theory and 3) Evolution. I won't go into detail about Evolution Theory and the Big Bang Theory because I already covered them in my book called "Monkey's Blood" *plus* we are not here to look at them. Neither one of those two theories has any type of rational explanation for how humans got here in the first place.

Alright, fine. Since this is a beginner's guide I will briefly tell you what these two, irrational theories try and tell us about human life. The Big Bang Theory says there was a huge explosion and somehow Earth just so happened to come from the big bang equipped with plants, ozone layer, dirt, water and somehow every other substance life needs to survive...all in the perfect ratios and chemical make-up.

If any of you have ever blown shit up, you will know those results are not realistic. Let's say I blow up somebody's house. You will find pieces of materials that made up that house scattered everywhere. If the house was brick, with a metal roof and walls made of drywall...you would find pieces of that shit spread all over the neighborhood. If there was a mysterious big-bang in the universe and planet Earth somehow ended up with an intact ozone layer, trees and water...that would mean those materials would be found scattered all over the universe; but they're not.

For the record, the Big Bang Theory has an explanation for how Earth was formed with no explanation for how life came to be on this planet; while the Evolution Theory does have an explanation for how life came to be on this planet with no explanation for how the Earth was formed. It's like having peanut butter and no jelly or jelly with no peanut butter with these two, kissing cousins of theory!

Evolution claims all life basically started from a one-cell "being" and that being began to multiply. As it multiplied, it somehow took on the different DNA types to become all the animals on Earth. From this exceptionally irrational process, monkeys are the animals evolutionist tell us continued to evolve and became humans. Why some monkeys stopped becoming humans and some just kept on with the human-evolution process has not been discussed or proven by evolutionists.

Let's get the train back on the track and focus on what my belief system says about Earth and life. The Creation Theory says God made the Universe. Stop right there. That is a rational claim. We all know humans did not make this Universe; so at the worst case scenario, we have to concede that something or someone who is not human made the Universe. The Creation Story says this non-human entity is God.

That one statement alone beats most theories out there. It gives us an entity that is non-human. The Big Bang and Evolution theories couldn't even provide us with that most basic of points. Now the creator of this Universe has a face. We know this entity has a thought process that we can't even begin to comprehend. Do you know how hard it is to make a planet? Most of us would have trouble making a tricky dish such as lasagna. We humans have been able to create some masterpieces like skyscrapers and remote-controlled drones that can fly over enemy territory and decide on the fly which type of munition to unload on the people, vehicles and different structures...but we haven't even come *close* to building a planet. This non-human entity has created thousands of planets and thousands of other celestial places and things that we can study and dissect but *not* recreate!

And there it is: the Creation Theory has given us a reasonable, non-human option named God as being the manufacturer of everything we see and don't see.

CHAPTER THREE

The Manufacturer's Rules.

When you produce something, you are called a "producer". A producer and manufacturer are basically the same thing. A manufacture produces a product. The Creation Theory claims God is the manufacturer of the Universe, seen and unseen. If you are a manufacturer, you are the one who knows how a thing is supposed to operate.

A guy named Henry Ford manufactured a product called a car. Who do you think knows the best way for a car to operate? Probably Henry Ford because he made it. He designed it to run on gasoline. That means if you decide to fill the gas tank with diesel fuel, it won't run properly.[1] Pick any product on the planet and a safe bet would be that the manufacturer knows what's best for it.

---

[1] Myles Munroe message provided examples similar to these.

Steve Jobs knows what an iPhone and all the Apple products can do because he designed them. In both of these examples, the manufacturer makes the rules for his product.

Transfer that logic to Earth and humans. We can all agree that's where we are at. We also can agree that a non-human entity manufactured, or created, Earth. The Creation Theory says God is that non-human manufacturer. If God is in fact the manufacturer, it only makes sense that He would have a set of rules as to how everything on this planet should operate. Oh yeah, can we also agree there is no "luck" when it comes to our planet. By that I mean, can we all agree water, dirt, the ozone layer and other essentials for life are unique to planet Earth? This is important because we now are logically agreeing somebody must have designed this place.

If you look back through history thousands of years ago, there are records of humans claiming to have some type of spiritual contact with God. There was a race of people called the

Israelites who claimed God communicated with them and gave them Laws of Operation on planet Earth. These laws, often called scriptures or Sacred Scripts, have been passed down for hundreds of generations. To keep things simple, we won't try and go into all the scientific aspects of the Universe God put into play such as gravity, light, water, etc. We will focus on the manufacturer's laws for humans.

There are hundreds of laws and stories of contact with God that are recorded in history. For our purpose, we want to test the efficiency of the manufacturer's laws. Like with the Henry Ford and the car example: the manufacturer gets respect and credibility based on how well adherence to his laws for the product work. If you were to go against Henry Ford's laws for the car and put diesel in it instead of gas, the engine would mess up and it wouldn't operate like he claimed it would; but to his credit, when the operator followed the manufacturer's laws and put gas in the engine, it ran properly and operated exactly how the manufacturer, Henry Ford, said it would. We respect him for producing a necessary product that does what it promises to do.

God created humans. We are some of His products. He has given us His laws on how to operate through spoken tradition and writings such as the Bible and other sacred scripts. Let's test them:

1. Don't steal. When you go against this law and steal, people get mad. There is greed involved with stealing and being greedy is not a good character trait to have in society. It's not right to take something from someone that does not belong to you. Following that law prevents anger, stealing, greed and sadness so I would say it's a good law.
2. Treat people how you want to be treated. Everyone wants to be treated fairly. When we are treated fairly, we are happy. When we are treated unfairly we get mad, sad and frustrated. Being treated

unfairly is not a good thing and it's not what we want; so I would say that's a good law.

3. Give 10% to the church.[2] A lot of us have subscriptions and/or memberships. It's important to pay into processes that we think are important. If you like guns and being able to protect yourself, you are likely to give to the NRA. If you like to work out, you are likely to pay for a gym membership. If you like the role of the church in society as a place that carries out God's will, you are likely to pay tithes to the church. That's a good law for many reasons: 1) it helps promote God's laws, 2) it keeps you in a spirit of contributing to something and 3) it's a way of showing honor and respect to the manufacturer.

4. Kids have to respect their parents *and* parents have to respect their kids. This law establishes respect for

---

[2] The church today is not how the church was supposed to be based on Jesus's description of it.

the kids and parents: in order to get respect you have to give it and in order to give respect you have to get it.

5. Don't cheat on your husband or wife, don't have sex with your uncle, aunt, mom, dad, brother, sister, step-son, step-daughter...and the list goes on. When you go against these laws, the result is a lifetime of anger, jealousy, murder, molestation and more. Therefore, I think God's basic sex laws all make sense. Of all God's laws, His sex laws are the ones most people rebel against and don't want to follow.

In general, you should look at God's laws for yourself and see if they make sense or not. Take a situation in life that is bad or has caused pain, disrespect or hurt. Then see if that situation went against God's laws or not. Be thorough with this step. Look at situations you are in as well as situations others have been in, both good and bad, and then decide for yourself whether or not the manufacturer's rules should be followed or not.

I went through this process for myself and that's what made me respect the manufacturer of the Universe known as God. My relationships with my kids have mostly been characterized as not good. The reason was I went against God's laws and had sex outside of marriage. I've been to jail and prison several times. If I was honest with myself, these "vacations" can be linked to me not obeying God's laws. My health isn't as good as it once. The reason was I went against God's laws to not get drunk or high. I almost got killed when I and a couple guys went to rob a well-connected gangster's house. Once again, I had almost gone against one of God's laws that said "don't steal". The list goes on. Go ahead and try it for yourself and you will most likely find an explanation for why you are where you are in life. (The good news is, if you dig a little deeper into this whole 'God's rules' thing, you will also find a list of ways you can change any position you are in in life at any point and time.)

CHAPTER FOUR

***It* needs a name.**

Everything needs a name from your dog to your hairstyle. The term used to describe an action that goes against God's laws is called "sinning" or "to sin". There. *It* has a name.

CHAPTER FIVE

Can we get rid of *it*?

In life, things come and go. We can make anything go *away* or control it once we understand the "Away Process". Water comes down in the form of rain and goes *away* in the form of evaporation. When someone breaks a law in society, they are placed *away* in a jail somewhere. Food enters your body in one form and goes *away* in a different form. Understanding the "Away Process" is important in life. It helps you make sense of things. Understanding the "Away Process" for sin is an important aspect of understanding life as you now are beginning to see it.

Sin is a bad thing. The results of sin are destructive in our personal, professional, spiritual and social lives. In order to make something destructive go *away*, you have to first look at how it came. Let's say you have a mice problem in your house. How do you make that situation go *away*? You have to answer two questions: 1) how did *it* get in, 2) what attracted *it* and 3) what's the most proven way to get rid of *it*?

In the mouse scenario, once we figure out that the mouse got in through a hole in the basement wall and it was attracted to the food you left open on the kitchen counter…all that's left to do is find the best way to get rid of it. Many manufacturers claim to have the best way to get rid of mice. Some work. Some don't. The best result typically has a proven track record over a long period of time. Putting peanut butter on a mouse trap might catch some mice; but using cheese is gonna get 'em every time. Knowing that, why would you continue to use peanut butter instead of cheese?

If you're looking for a lawyer, you want one with lots of experience in the area you need help with. If you have a problem with your heart, you don't just need any doctor: you need a heart doctor and it is best if he has lots of experience.

The issue of getting rid of sin and the resulting destruction in your life is more important than the issues in those two examples; but the process is the same. You need to figure out, 1) how did sin get in, 2) what attracted sin and 3) what's the most proven way to get rid of sin?

Let's take Point #1. According to the Creation Theory, sin came into existence in the very beginning when humans first went against God's laws. Since Adam was the first human, he gets the rap for allowing sin into the world. As history records show, Adam's wife Eve was tempted by Satan to do something that went against God's laws. Adam followed her lead and he also sinned. <u>Since God created Adam first, God placed the blame on him because He felt Adam should have known better.</u> The underlined part is a very important point in gaining a general understanding of the "Away Process". From that point on, all humans had sin in their nature.

That leads us to Point #2. What is it about sin that humans are attracted to? Freedom. The ability to make your own rules and live life how you want is an attractive thing. Society teaches us that you can create your own destiny: all you have to do is focus on what you want to be in life and you can be it. People are so lost in the world right now that an entire industry of life coaches, or people who generally like to give motivational speeches, are raking in billions of dollars by doing one thing: telling you that you can do anything you want and that you can get whatever you want out of life by simply challenging your energy towards your goal. They make it all about you and people love to hear that. People love the idea that our destinies and purpose for living is not left in the hands of some God or *thing* nobody has ever seen. It gives us faith in us and in each other...and it takes faith and focus away from the Manufacturer's rules.

The act of sinning was and is attractive to humans because it allows us to make our own rules and live life how we want to live them. God, the manufacturer, wanted us to live by His rules for our good. In fact, the ability to describe and live out your own set of rules is what most people consider life is all about. We even attempt to make things legal that God and the Bible say are illegal.

This attraction to doing our own thing and believing in the human race and our systems as being the rules for how life should be lived is constantly reinforced in the media. We love movies where somebody is poor and they work hard and achieve their purpose in life against all odds. They become our heroes.

Going down the path where we acknowledge our own sets of laws has proven to be very destructive. White people made laws to legally enslave black people. Rich businessmen make laws to avoid paying taxes so they can hoard billions of dollars for themselves. Some states say consensual sex is age 15 while others say 18. Some places say it's legal to have sex with animals while some say it's not. Money is used to break established laws in the name of corporate greed…and the list goes on.

Doing your thing by your rules has proven itself to be destructive in all areas of life. People are looking for solutions from the destructiveness of sin in sin. Let me make that simple: Sin is the result of going against God's laws with our own, individual, man-made laws. Once we see destruction or prejudice that is the result of certain practices, we still resort to making other man-made laws to fix things with no regard for the Manufacturer's laws and wonder why our problems still exist.

Point #3 is "what's the most proven way to get rid of sin?" Since we have freewill, we have a choice. We can continue to try and find man-made releases from sin or we can try something *new* and follow the Manufacturer's process for getting rid of sin.

The Bible and other Sacred Scripts record the Manufacturer's "Away Process" to get rid of sin: a blood sacrifice. I'll keep the blood sacrifice simple so you can see how logical it is. Adam and Eve did not experience death until they sinned. Once they sinned, death now became the punishment. When you die, your blood "spills out". Early scriptures show us that God is all about the legal process and since humans sinned, they had to die. That means every time you sin you must die. God found a solution: spill the blood of something innocent to cover the life of humans.

In other words, when you sin, instead of you dying, you can sacrifice something that hasn't sinned like a baby cow or sheep, and that innocent blood shed will cover your sins. Legally, a sin was committed and was paid for in death (spilled blood)...just not human blood. This process stayed in existence for thousands of years. It was quite a messy, stinky process as you can imagine. It would be illogical to have us humans offer a blood sacrifice every time we sinned, so God instructed humans to offer a blood sacrifice once at the end of the year. That sacrifice was sufficient and realistic enough to legally cover last year's sins.

The Manufacturer was content with that type of sacrifice because if checked off all legal requirements of death/spilled blood, and allowed humans to live out their purpose on Earth without somebody dying every 15 seconds from sinning.

Without getting too technical, I will just say the Manufacturer in this case had a Son. His son's name has been translated to Jesus in the English language. Stay with me. I won't get super spiritual and technical. Watch this:

1. God had a son named Jesus
2. Jesus loves His Father and the Father loves His son
3. The son sees how messed up His Father's creation has become and is willing to do whatever it takes to make

things right. The only thing that can legally make things right is for a human's blood be sacrificed instead of a perfect animal; because it was initially a human who sinned so a human must die/spill blood.

4. The son agrees and dies/spills His blood; becoming that perfect human sacrifice that was needed to legally die/spill blood to restore the destruction of sin. Remember the underlined part I mentioned earlier about how through one man sin legally had power over humans? Well, since that's true, legally through one man sin can go *away* and no longer have power over humans.[3]

5. Humans now legally have power over sin again. This power comes from recognizing, understanding and having faith in what Jesus did.

6. How many of us children wouldn't want to do whatever it took to restore a family business or to keep a family

---
[3] Romans 5:12

together? Jesus did what any son/child would do to preserve the family business or to reunite the family.

This is a beginner's guide to sinning and sin so there is no need for me to try and take this restoration process to a whole 'nother level of understanding and use big spiritual words. The main take away is this: look at the 6 steps you just read. If you can look at them and see how it kind of makes sense, then you have graduated from being a beginner to whatever step is just above that. On the other hand, if you looked at the 6 steps you just read and aren't able to connect the dots, you are still a beginner and this book is truly for you, buddy. No big deal. It just means you have to go back to page one and read this guide until you are able to see the logic in those 6 steps and *then* you can proceed to digging into the Bible and other Sacred Scripts to take your understanding of how Jesus' life and death are directly related to your happiness and success in life.

CHAPTER SIX

Now what?

At the end of Chapter 5, we have established that it is crucial for you to grasp the basics of the 6 points mentioned there before you should move on. If you are in the position to move forward, your "now what?" involves you applying the "Away Process" to as many areas of your life as possible. Even if you don't understand the legal power you have because of what Jesus did, apply the three "Away Process" questions to any situation in your life and you will begin to see the relevance and pure brilliance of God's laws.

In life there are laws for everything. We make laws for the enjoyment and productivity of society; so why is that so hard to accept God's laws? As the Manufacturer, His goal is to make sure humans enjoy his product and are as productive as possible. The

Manufacturer knows your purpose. Have you ever listened to those life coaches and motivational speakers and still been stuck in the mud? That's because they didn't create you so they can't tell you how to live out your purpose.

I follow the 10-Point Must system to gauge how well I am following my purpose based on God's laws and I also use it to determine how happy I will be at any given moment. Those of you who aren't familiar with this system, it is a scoring system used in boxing and mixed-martial-arts fighting. At the end of each round of fighting, each judge must give one fighter a score of "10" and the other fighter a number less than "10". How much farther down from "10" is based on how less effective the lower-scoring fighter competed. In a close fight, a judge may score a round 10-9. In a round where there was a clear winner, the score may look more like 10-6.

You start off and give yourself a "10" score. This means you are following God's laws 100% making your score "100". Now take a look at your life as it relates to God's laws. There's a law that says, "don't lie". How well are you doing with that? If that is a major problem area, subtract 10 from your score; but if it is a mild problem area of sin, take off 5. Now you are operating at either 90 or 95% productivity in life and should still be pretty happy. Do this for all areas in your life, adding 10 for God's laws where you are very strong at and 5 where you are still doing pretty good at it. This scoring system is your personal success tracker! Make this scoring system your Guiding Light…your North Star!

I came up with this system to help me relax in life and see what I should be expecting from life. When one of my addictions was getting the best of me, I would tell myself I was losing that round with a 10-3 score. That "3" score let me know it was gonna be a long, unproductive, miserable-ass day unless I got back in the fight and raised that "3" to at *least* a "6". I knew the closer I could get to "10", the more happy I would be. It required that I apply the Manufacturer's Rules better in my life and in *that* sense, yes, I was able to live out my purpose in life and so can you.

The "10-Point Must System" is the key to finding your true purpose and success in every area of your life!

CHAPTER SEVEN

Private Matters

This section is in the back of every book in the series. It shows different views on issues like abortion, drugs, sex, politics, religion and other topics people only talk about in private; making these issues Private Matters. Take a look and see how you feel and learn to see there are at least two different views on any given subject; but only one that really matters: the Manufacturer's.

1. Porn Industry 101 39

2. Cross-Cultural Advantage 44

3. My Nigga 50

PORN INDUSTRY 101

The porn industry is a home-wrecker/relationship killer. The porn industry is a career-killer. The porn industry is manhood-killer. How do I know? Because I used to love porn and everything attached to it: sexual fantasy life, sex drugs, sex, drugs...

From reading the different stories in the Bible you can see how sex and lust affected many people's lives negatively...just like it does today. It made King David, a great Man of God, commit 1st degree murder. A King was willing to give up half of his kingdom for a lap dance. These may be situations that occurred a long time ago, but I am sure we all know, or are that person, who has made some dumb decisions because we allowed sex and lust to be the deciding factors.

The porn industry is an industry that faithfully reaps in several billion dollars a year with no signs of slowing down. IF YOU DO NOT GET A HANDLE ON YOUR SEXUAL DESIRES AND EXPECTATIONS, THIS INDUSTRY WILL CONTINUE TO TEAR UP HOME LIVES AND KILL DREAMS.

Sex sells. I have seen commercials for cookies that show a sexxxy female dancing around with some tight, fitting jeans on and some cleavage showing talking about how much she loves milk and cookies. I am lactose intolerant and I almost went out to buy some milk and cookies because they made it seem like if I presented a snack of milk and cookies to a female that she would somehow, in anticipation of me bringing here this snack, be waiting around in some sexxxy jeans or a nice short skirt, eagerly awaiting my phone call letting her know I was on the way with her favorite: milk and cookies.

Lucky for you, we are about to pull back the curtain and see how this industry can, and needs to be, brought to its knees. As a man, I can only give it to you from a man's point of view; and to be more specific I can only share my point of view. And to keep things simple, I will use the term "porn-activity" to refer to watching pornos, strippers and dabbling with escorts/prostitutes interchangeably. Here's how it got me:

Home Wrecker/Relationship Killer – Porn activity females are not portraying their nurturing, wifely, motherly sides. They show every side *except* those sides. This all appears harmless enough, but the more you watch and get involved, the more you begin to view women as simply sex objects. And why not??? They appear to be so happy and willing and as a man, you naturally want to make a female happy.

1. The more accustomed to fantasy women, the less I was able to deal with a real woman. I was able to have all my basic female needs taken care of without all the talking and commitment.
2. Women I talked to said they would never consider marriage to a man who was involved in porn-activity because they know they can't compete with a female in that industry.
3. I got addicted to cocaine. Drugs and alcohol put you in a state of temporary "happiness". Cocaine kept my fantasy sex life alive; while killing any hopes of having a real sex life.
4. The more my failures at having a real relationship grew because of my drug addiction and shame, the more my attempts to get in relationships did long-lasting damage to my girlfriends and the children that were the result of these relationships.

Career Killer – Having a career for me was out of the question. For each person this may be different. I allowed porn-activity to kill my career dreams and goals because of my inability to deal with real life.

1. I longed to be in a relationship so bad that I got high to enjoy my fantasy relationship any chance I could. Having a career and a drug addiction don't mix.
2. It became harder and harder for me to see myself in a real career achieving real results when I had no confidence in my dealings with reality.
3. It's hard to realize your dreams of being a big-time business owner and investor when you spend your savings on porn-related activities.

Manhood Killer – Becoming a man, like anything else in life, is the results of your habits. My habits were stripping me of my confidence and manhood with each bad decision.

1. A man respects a woman. The porn industry teaches men to treat women with disrespect, wanting them only as sex objects.
2. A man knows how to handle reality. The porn industry teaches men to sacrifice reality for fantasy.
3. A man knows how to budget his finances. Budgeting money for sexual fantasies is not practical or wise.

4. A man loves commitment. The porn industry wants men to constantly be on the lookout for new and exciting sexual experiences.

There is a point in your life where it becomes harder to go back to the way it was. Kind of like a cucumber: once it becomes a pickle...it can't be a cucumber anymore. Your life is the sum results of habits. Someone acted towards you based on the habits they were taught or you acted the way you did based on your habits.

The Bible teaches us and shows us and warns us about sex. There are plenty of examples that show the goods and the bads. Sex was designed to be a beautiful act that compliments the natural attraction between a man and a woman to create children. We wouldn't be here without it. Our ability to enjoy life depends on our ability to enjoy sex the way it was meant to be. The BIBLE: Basic Instructions Before Leaving Earth...about sex. That's my new view and I'm stickin' to it.

CROSS-CULTURAL ADVANTAGE

Culture is a major part of being human. It is, at bare minimum, the common link between any two people. It gives a person pride in their country. It gives any given group in society a feeling of purpose and accomplishment. Culture is what gives you a basis for your existence. Cultural festivals are proud moments for anyone of the group being celebrated; especially when the celebration is world-wide. For people without cultural identity, any cultural benefits are un-applicable to you. Characteristics of people in "culture-less" groups tend to be lack of motivation, anger, jealousy, stress, depression, isolation, self-hatred and their actions typically appear to have been programmed and controlled by negative outside forces.

The highest levels of joy and beauty in life can only be found in opposites. You appreciate summer's heat after experiencing winter's cool. You appreciate and strive for the feeling of being loved and acknowledged more so after being hated and ignored. Seeing the sun sets your mind on a different mentality after being able to shutdown and relax hours earlier under the cloak of darkness. Humanity began and exists because of opposites: the sexual actions and differences of a man and a woman. When you have no other connections to humans and feel isolated it's gratifying to be able to know and build on cultural connections to give you that feeling of being a part of something.

Culture is a major part of being human. It is, at bare minimum, the common link between any two people. When that bare minimum desire of humanity does not exist, purpose in life gets distorted.

The Bible introduces us to a new culture. A culture that is 100% positive. Something that is 100% means there is no room for anything else. It is full. It is complete; and in the case of the cross culture there is no room for negativity such as lack of motivation, anger, jealousy, stress, depression, isolation and self-hatred. This culture is symbolized by the cross: the act of Jesus dying on the cross. That act introduced us to the only culture that matters.

Being a part of the Cross Culture has benefits with no liabilities. When you are a part of that culture, you interact with people differently. You don't judge someone based on their appearance, because you understand appearances don't determine achievable elevation in life. You understand that *everyone* has the same seed-potential as you. You are governed by laws that transcend every manmade law that is not based on or enforced with love.

The only outside influences in this culture is God. Your understanding of and getting into relationship with God is what gives members of this culture an advantage over any other cultural group. Every cultural group except for Cross Culture is limited by ethnicity or acceptance by a member of a certain ethnicity. Cross Culture is only limited by humanity without distinction. Meaning, each member is a distinct, valuable member of this culture with the only qualification being that you are a human.

Worldly kings and queens are crowned based on money and bloodlines. Cross Culture kings and queens are crowned at birth regardless of their economic status or bloodline at birth. Cross

Culture members have the inalienable right by birth to be the first in a line of royalty in their bloodline at any point and time in their life. Cross Culture kings and queens are proclaimed royalty by the creator of the universe...not by the amount of wealth his family has or by the inherited status of his or her parents. Money can be manipulated and so can royalty that is based on it; bloodlines have no bearing in determining admission to royalty of a Cross Culture member.

A Cross Culture member is only limited in life by his or her view on what Jesus did by dying on the cross: Your view matters.

MY NIGGA

People say I belong to the cultural group called either Black or African American or Afro American or Negro. Members of this (or technically "these") cultural groups have their own rationale for why they prefer the term they chose. What's the importance of finding the politically correct term at all? And how does the word "nigga" fit into this picture?

Here's how. Humans love to be a part of something. It doesn't matter what cultural or religious group you are in, you want to be a part of something. Kids shoot up their schools as a result of not fitting in. Politicians vote against common sense just to fit in with their political party. Police officers remain silent while their fellow co-workers inflict harm on the people they are sworn to protect because they want to remain part of the police union. It's human nature.

When Africans came to the United States through the slave trade, white people who were linked to the slave trade here were taught how to get the best "results" and compliance from their slaves. All of the methods that were taught, and then consequently passed down through the generations, dealt with isolation.

The African slaves constantly had their lives and families forcibly and intentionally disrupted and kept in a constant state of fear. This was backed up by the Constitution of the United States as well as the majority of courthouse rulings in America. State, Federal and Local law enforcement also routinely used violence, often times lethal violence, to "legally" keep up this disruptive practice and state of confusion.

Common tactics were to have the kids of slave couples being sold off to different plantations. They were forced to not use their native African languages. They weren't allowed to learn how to read English. Everything that was inflicted on black people was intentionally and deceptively designed to not let them unite as a cultural group. Being part of a cultural group is a symbol of humanity. In order for white America to continue to benefit from slave activity, black people had to be denied a specific, legitimate cultural identity...forcing them into sub-human status in American society.

And this is where the word "nigga" fits in. Regardless to your complexion (light or dark), you were considered to be a nigga. White Americans began with legitimate terms from other languages that meant black such as negro and niger. In the end, they settled for the term nigga and nigger.

And there it is: Africans that were transplanted to America as slaves suddenly found themselves with a name that was recognized, used and identified them as a group no matter where they went in America. They were now officially nigga's or nigger's.

As is typical with human nature, black people now began to identify themselves and other members of this new "cultural group" by nigga. It began to take on an eerie, yet affectionate, tone. This was the underlying result of belonging. Black people now "belonged" in America as a "legitimate" cultural group.

The problem is that black people had this term forced on them. In the eyes of most white people and the courts, this term represented everything negative about humanity. It was bad enough that blacks had to start off legally in American society as sub-humans. They now had to carry this label with them and somehow make it work. They made it work too good.

The passion, the closeness, the pain of being labeled a curse yet feeling like a blessing, the genuine familial bonds that were forged behind this word all made it seem attractive. The realness of the need to want to be a part of something to the point where you take on the worst possible label and surviving is captivating.

Making it through the legal challenges and persecutions, rapings, lynchings and beatings showed a resilience that people want to identify with. This mental fortitude and strength of black Americans, just like the generational frame of mind that white Americans passed onto their children, was as legitimate as any other culture's passing of generational ways.

    Black people who use the word nigga use it and accept the good and bad elements of it without shame. White people who use the word nigga either use it because of the magnetism of its realness or as a pitiful expression of racism that has no sting, trauma-tied experience or generationally taught power over people of this generation or the previous one...or future one's.

It is my opinion that real seeks real. Unity seeks unity. Human bonding is universal. If using the word nigga feels right in your soul...use it. If it doesn't...then don't. Anyone who uses this term that is not black must use it "responsibly". That means they must understand all aspects of the origins of the word, and if they are using it, they need to understand that they are publicly pledging their allegiance and real support to any cause that seeks to unjustly target persons of this "culture".

Any black person who has not directly been affected by the physical and mental persecution and horror of slavery and racism during the time in American history where the word nigga held the lethal power of a bullet should not be offended. This word united your ancestors. This word symbolized the power of human nature to survive. This word did not break the resolve of your uprooted culture and this word will not break you either, my nigga.

That is my view.

Personal Development Plan Notes

Personal Development Plan Notes

Personal Development Plan Notes

Personal Development Plan Notes

Personal Development Plan Notes

Personal Development Plan Notes

Personal Development Plan Notes

Personal Development Plan Notes

Personal Development Plan Notes

Personal Development Plan Notes

Personal Development Plan Notes

Personal Development Plan Notes

Personal Development Plan Notes

Personal Development Plan Notes

Personal Development Plan Notes

Personal Development Plan Notes

Personal Development Plan Notes

Personal Development Plan Notes

Personal Development Plan Notes

Personal Development Plan Notes